SLEEP

SLEEP

50 MINDFULNESS AND RELAXATION EXERCISES FOR A RESTFUL NIGHT

DR. ARLENE K. UNGER

METRO BOOKS
New York

METRO BOOKS
New York

An Imprint of Sterling Publishing Co., Inc.
1166 Avenue of the Americas
New York, NY 10036

This book is not intended as a substitute for medical or
psychotherapeutic advice, and readers are advised to consult a healthcare
professional for individual concerns and to check that the exercises are
suitable for their particular needs. The creators of the work and the
publisher cannot be held liable for any actions that may be taken as
a consequence of the information in this book.

ISBN 978-1-4351-6662-2

For information about custom editions, special sales,
and premium and corporate purchases, please contact Sterling
Special Sales at 800-805-5489 or specialsales@sterlingpublishing.com.

Manufactured in China by Toppan Leefung Printers Limited

2 4 6 8 10 9 7 5 3 1

www.sterlingpublishing.com

Credits: Kerry Enzor; Therefore Publishing Limited;
Philippa Davis; Zarni Win

MIX
Paper from
responsible sources
FSC® C104723

CONTENTS

INTRODUCTION

Sleep is something of a mystery. Given how much of our lives is given over to sleeping, we understand remarkably little about its processes or its functions. But we do know that we cannot go for long without feeling the need to sleep. We also know that we see sleep as one of life's pleasures, even though—paradoxically—we are more or less unconscious when we experience it. And we feel instinctively that sleep does our minds and bodies profound good.

Generally, the brain seems to use the hours of sleep to run various subroutines (to borrow from the language of computing). It sorts and analyzes new knowledge, solves problems, and makes strategies. This is certainly why babies sleep more than adults—because they have so much more data to deal with relative to their experience. And it is surely also why we sometimes wake to find that we have the answer to a predicament that has been vexing us. "Sleeping on it" is a fruitful problem-solving ploy.

Why do we need sleep?
We are primed to ensure that we get sleep when we need it. To put it another way, the human body is designed to read signals in the external world, and to relay them to the brain in a way that makes us feel sleepy. Our internal messenger is melatonin, a hormone that is secreted when we find ourselves in darkness. The effect of melatonin is not just to send us to sleep at regular

intervals, but also to align our body clocks with the onset of night-time. All other things being equal, we sleep when it is dark, and wake up when it gets light (because daylight turns off the production of melatonin). We can override this hormonal signal if we want to—but if we keep going against the natural sleep pattern, this tends to have an impact over time. Shiftworkers are notoriously prone to sleep problems and modern technology, which permits us to spend our evenings in brightly lit rooms or staring at bright screens, is at the root of many a sleep disorder.

Sleep strategies

The good news is that sleep problems are treatable. It need not be a question of taking medication (though that may sometimes be appropriate); more often than not, all that a person suffering from sleep problems needs is a range of strategies to deal with disturbances when they occur.

This book contains 50 such strategies. Many of these involve "visualizations." Professional sports people have long used a literal form of visualization: they try vividly to see themselves making that hole in one, or scoring that penalty, before actually having to do it. As for the rest of us, recent brain studies support the notion that mental imagery has a positive effect on our ability to plan, perceive, focus, and control our actions.

The exercises in this book are drawn from three psychotherapeutic techniques. They are emotional brain training, cognitive behavioral therapy, and mindfulness-based stress reduction, which can be successfully used in conjunction with each other.

When to see a doctor
Many sleep problems can be resolved by self-help measures such as those outlined in this book. But if your sleep problems continue or if you experience loud snoring, acid reflux, restless legs, sleep talking, sleepwalking, or other symptoms when you are asleep, consult a doctor for individual advice. Sleeping difficulties can be a symptom of other health problems, which may need medical attention.

THE FIVE STAGES OF SLEEP

Sleep is not a uniform state of being, but a cycle of five different stages. This cycle takes about 90 minutes to complete, so we go through the sleep cycle four to six times a night. These are the stages:

1 **Light sleep:** at the start of the cycle. Muscle activity decreases, but twitching may occur. Light sleep is when we are most likely to wake up.

2 **Real sleep:** when we become properly unconscious, and so are disconnected from our physical environment. Breathing and heart rate are regular, but body temperature begins to fall.

3 **Deep sleep:** when the body is totally relaxed, and blood pressure drops. We might be unresponsive to noise or other external activity. At this stage our brains produce delta waves, a kind of high-amplitude brain activity. These are known to stimulate growth hormones and are thought to be instrumental in the formation of memories during sleep.

4 **Restorative sleep:** when our heart and breathing rate is at its lowest. Hormones are secreted that promote cell growth and muscle development; this is when the body repairs itself. Experiments have shown that wounds heal more quickly during sleep than wakefulness.

5 **REM sleep:** when our eyes dart back and forth beneath the lids—REM stands for "rapid eye movement"—and we appear to be "watching" some kind of scene. As indeed we are, since REM sleep is when we dream. If we wake during REM sleep we can usually recall the content of the interrupted dream. If we are woken at other points in the cycle, we usually have no memory of having dreamed.

Positive affirmations

Throughout the book you'll find a number of positive affirmations. These are short phrases that you can repeat in order to reinforce a message in your subconscious mind and which encourage you to develop positive perceptions of yourself.

Emotional brain training

According to emotional brain training (or EBT), many of the things that cause us stress are located in what practitioners call the emotional brain. Emotional brain training teaches that it is possible to identify and rewire negative feelings and return to more positive feelings through a process known as "cycling" and through self-regulation. With sleep issues, emotional brain training aims to dampen negative emotional stress while encouraging people to find reward in being still and letting the body heal through the night. Emotional brain training also confronts the self-defeating patterns that might keep a person from pursuing healthy exercise, diet, and lifestyle, all of which promote better sleep.

Cognitive behavioral therapy

Often referred to as CBT, this therapy is used to treat a wide range of problems—depression, addiction, anxiety—by giving patients incremental steps toward positive changes. Its main function is to help people understand how their thoughts and emotions impact their behavior. By identifying and modifying dysfunctional patterns of thinking and feeling, patients learn to positively influence their behavior. Cognitive behavioral therapy improves sleep by showing people how to replace negative thoughts with positive ones, and by changing pre-bedtime habits. It also teaches stress-reduction techniques and promotes a healthy lifestyle.

Mindfulness-based stress reduction (MBSR)

This therapy combines mindfulness meditation with yoga-related teachings. Mindfulness is derived from Buddhist thinking, but in its modern form it is nonspiritual. It is a method for observing one's mental patterns and behaviors in a detached, interested way. Mindfulness means focusing totally on what is happening now, because the now is all there is (the past is gone; and the future hasn't happened). It also means not forming judgments about oneself ("I'm doing it wrong, I'm so dumb…"). Mindfulness-based stress reduction can reduce stress in people who are too overwhelmed, worried, or depressed to sleep.

This book encourages you to try out all three approaches, and some exercises draw on more than one approach. Take the time to test the different exercises and adopt the ones that work best for you. Experiment and, if you like, adapt the imagery of the visualizations to suit your personal preferences. Before long you will reap the benefits that come from a calmer mind and long and peaceful sleep.

Below: Bringing to mind soothing images, such as this sleeping cat, can help to trigger feelings of relaxation and provide a useful gateway to sleep.

SLEEP
MATTERS

About a third of American adults are bothered by sleeplessness, according to the US National Institutes of Health. That's a big problem. Stress, bringing work into the bedroom, a night-time obsession with electronic games or social media, and keeping erratic schedules have led to sleeplessness reaching epidemic proportions.

Cognitive behavioral therapists and other sleep experts say that all of us can improve our sleep by adopting good "sleep hygiene." This rather clinical expression means nothing more than preparing for sleep as you would for any other important activity. So you should ensure that your bedroom is conducive to sleep, that you have a restful evening, and that you avoid excessive alcohol or heavy foods, which might end up disturbing your night. In this chapter you will find exercises and advice drawn from cognitive behavioral therapy, emotional brain training, and mindfulness. Together they will help you to adopt a more sleep-friendly lifestyle and create an evening routine that leads naturally to deep, restful sleep.

01 LOVE THE DARK

Nothing is more likely to induce sleepiness than being in the dark. It is not facetious to say that night-time is nature's way of telling us to go to bed, because when darkness comes we naturally produce the sleep-inducing hormone melatonin. Here are three different ways to embrace the dark.

1 Keep the lights down low in the evening. Switch on soft lamps rather than full overhead lighting, and use a dimmer switch if you have one.

2 While sitting in a darkened room, listen to some soft and restful music. Try making a playlist of evening music to enjoy. You can also try doing a mindful breathing exercise or some gentle yoga stretches in a dimly lit room.

3 If it is winter and already dark outside, make this a reason for an early night. Otherwise, while sitting comfortably, do a simple night visualization: imagine the cool stillness of the night air, the stars in their allotted places in the heavens, a crescent moon making its stately progress across the sky.

WHEN TO DO IT

Make a little bit of dark time part of your nightly routine. Your body will learn to take the hint, and it will help to make you feel sleepy before you go to bed.

02 RIVER OF RELAXATION

Many of us are so wound up during our waking hours that we don't even know how to get our bodies to relax. Yet creating a sense of physical relaxation in the body is important for sleep. This progressive relaxation technique comes from cognitive behavioral therapy. It works through the body, first creating tension and then releasing the tension in each muscle group in turn. This teaches us how to prime our bodies for relaxation.

1 Find a comfortable chair to sit in. You can do this exercise lying down but you are likely to drift off to sleep and the aim here is to learn to relax the body when you are awake.

2 Close your eyes and take a few deep breaths before you start. Focus on the muscles in your hands. Take a breath and squeeze both fists tightly. Hold for 5 seconds.

3 As you exhale, release your grip and let the tension flow out of your hands like a river flowing downstream. Continue to breathe, focusing on that sense of release for 5 seconds.

WHEN TO DO IT

Practice this exercise for 10 minutes before bed and after waking up each day. Notice how it reduces your stress level and releases your built-up body tension. By making this exercise a habit, you'll sleep better and wake up without the physical effects of anxiety.

4 Now you are ready to do the tensing and relaxing with the other muscle groups, starting with your toes. Curl them down for 5 seconds on the inhale and on the exhale let them release, keeping the idea of water cascading out as you do so and noticing how this feels for 5 seconds.

5 Now work upward through the body, tensing each muscle group for 5 seconds and then releasing and noticing for 5 seconds. Do your lower legs (gently raise your toes upward to create tension in the calf), your thighs, buttocks, abdomen, chest (take a deep breath in to tense the muscles), arms, shoulders, and neck (raise the shoulders upward), and then your mouth, eyes (shut them tightly), and forehead (raise your eyebrows).

6 Take a few moments to notice how loose and relaxed your body feels after doing the exercise.

7 Once you are well practiced in this exercise, consider dropping the tensing part and just work with mentally priming your muscles to relax.

HOW TO HELP

This can be a useful exercise for managing anxiety, but at first try to do it when you are calm—it is easier to learn that way, and once it becomes a habit you can use it whenever you feel anxious or tense.

I enjoy
the sensation
of
release

SANCTUARY FOR SLEEP

03

Your bedroom might be one factor that is stopping you getting a proper night's rest, according to sleep scientists. This exercise calls for you to apply the emotional brain-training tool of sanctuary to your bedroom, which should be as inviting and restful as a tropical beach.

1 When you have an hour to spare, go to your bedroom and look on it as if for the first time.

2 Is it a tidy space? If not, do something about that. Make the bed, put clothes away in the closet, and find a place for anything that doesn't belong here.

3 Is it a peaceful space? If you can hear noise from outside, think what you can do. Thick curtains are effective at reducing noise as well as light.

4 Is it a comfortable space? When did you last change the mattress or buy new pillows? Replace them if they are showing signs of wear.

5 Is it a restful space? Make sure that any light is blocked out when the curtains or blinds are drawn. You sleep better in a very dark room.

WHEN TO DO IT

Choose a day each week to evaluate your sleep sanctuary. Look for what needs to be thrown out, given away, kept, or left in sight. See how much better you sleep and feel when your bedroom reflects the calmness you deserve.

04 BEDTIME FOODS

One of the main causes of sleeplessness is overeating in the evening. So you should aim to have your evening meal at least three hours before going to bed. If that leaves you so hungry at bedtime that it affects your sleep, then it is a good idea to have a late evening snack with sleep-inducing properties—try these ideas.

1 A glass of warmed milk; this really does help you feel sleepy because it contains the amino acid tryptophan, which aids in the production of the sleep hormone melatonin. And since warm milk reminds us of being a baby, it subconsciously evokes feelings of relaxation and comfort.

2 Other foods that contain tryptophan include oats, bananas, and turkey. Try a small turkey sandwich or an oatmeal bar. It's good to have a few carbs in the evening—they have been shown to help the brain access tryptophan.

3 Or go for a handful of cherries or a glass of tart cherry juice—cherries are rich in melatonin. One study found that drinking cherry juice helped increase participants' sleep by 25 minutes.

WHEN TO DO IT

Whenever you need to! Be careful not to oversnack and so make yourself too full to sleep. Avoid any stimulants such as alcohol and caffeine—coffee, black tea, and chocolate. It's best not to drink any liquid in large quantities before bedtime to avoid night-time trips to the bathroom.

05 FIT FOR SLEEP

It's well known that getting plenty of exercise helps to promote sleep. So make a point of getting the recommended 30 minutes of activity a day, five days a week. This can be broken up into shorter chunks of 10 minutes or more if you find that easier to manage. Here is how to maximize the sleep benefits from your fitness routine.

1 Keep intense exercise sessions for the daytime. Doing vigorous exercise within three hours of bedtime can make it harder to get to sleep because your body doesn't have a chance to cool down. Instead, try doing meditative forms of exercise such as yoga or tai chi in the evening.

2 Make a point of walking each and every day. Daytime walking is best as it increases the amount of natural sunlight the body receives.

3 Try walking attentively and mindfully: make a point of noticing how your body feels, and what is going on around you. Make a mental list of interesting things, people, or incidents you see along the way. This gives your brain as well as your body a workout, which encourages it to switch to rest mode in the evening.

WHEN TO DO IT

Try to build walking into your daily routine. Could you walk to or from work, at least a couple of times a week? Could you walk your children to school rather than take the car?

06   LEAVE WORK BEHIND

This exercise is inspired by cognitive behavioral therapy, and encourages you to treat leftover work thoughts like mosquitoes buzzing in your ear. Just like mosquitoes, our thoughts can be annoyances that interfere with our ability to relax. Here are three ways to keep them out of the bedroom.

1 If you drive home, pause at the end of your journey. Visualize your work thoughts as mosquitoes or other noisy bugs and watch them fly into the glove compartment. Shut them in and leave them until the next day.

2 If your "mosquitoes" are really bugging you, then try giving yourself time to attend to them. Set a time limit—half an hour, say—after which you will leave all work worries until the following day.

3 If your mosquito thoughts still won't give you peace, take them elsewhere. Go for a walk, or sit in a park. Perhaps you will find, when you come home, that you have left them behind.

WHEN TO DO IT

Practice this exercise when you arrive home from work each day. With time, you will learn to let what happens at work stay at work.

07 GIVE THANKS

As bedtime approaches, try doing this simple gratitude exercise to remind yourself of some of the things you appreciate. Studies show that writing down what you are grateful for can have a positive effect on the quality and duration of your sleep. In other words, if your heart is thankful, you get a better night's rest.

1 Take a few minutes to be by yourself, and concentrate on the exercise. You will need a notebook and pen.

2 Take a few breaths, and be still. Then, when you are ready, write down something that is a source of gratitude. It can be something beautiful that you have noticed today—such as flowers growing by the roadside—or a transient thing such as some small act of kindness of which you were on the receiving end. Or it can be a major factor in your life such as your health or the love and support of your family.

3 Once you have noted three reasons to be grateful, take a couple more minutes to be still and breathe before starting your night-time routine.

WHEN TO DO IT

If you do this exercise every evening, your general sense of well-being as well as your sleep should improve—and you will end up with a humbling and fascinating journal of thankfulness.

TOP **FIVE** WAYS
to help sleep

Enjoy active days and
plenty of daylight

Keep the later part
of your evenings calm

Make your bedroom
a restful place to be

Have a consistent
bedtime and rising time

Avoid caffeine and other
stimulants in the evening

08 KEEP A CLEAN SHEET

There is no doubt that a bed that feels fresh and unrumpled is more conducive to sleep. But for many people, making the bed is way down on the list of morning priorities. Cognitive behavioral therapy teaches that people are more likely to change their ways if they come up with clear "reinforcements" for acting differently. So here is a list of reinforcements to help you remember why you should try to make your bed at the start of each day.

1 It signifies the end of your sleep time and the beginning of your work day.

2 It gives you a sense of completion when you leave your bedroom.

3 It gets you into the mode of accomplishing things throughout your day.

4 It invites you to a quieter bedtime and a calmer sleep at night.

WHEN TO DO IT

Commit these benefits to memory and remind yourself of them every day. A small thing such as a tidy bed can make a big difference to your life.

09 UP WITH THE ROOSTER

If you sleep in on the weekend, try this exercise to reset your body clock. According to cognitive behavioral therapists and other sleep experts, having a regular sleep–wake cycle—going to bed and getting up at the same time seven days a week—is a key component of good sleep hygiene. A study published by the American Psychological Association found early risers to be happier, healthier, and more successful than those who sleep in.

1 Ask yourself why you "need" to get up earlier? It can help to have an enjoyable reason: practicing a short yoga session, packing a lunch (rather than buying it in), or giving yourself 10 minutes to write a letter to a friend. Make a note of your reason and put it beside your bed as a reminder.

2 Set your alarm clock for 15 minutes earlier than today. Don't use a device with a snooze button, and make sure that it is out of reach—so that you can't turn it off without getting out of bed.

3 Keep giving yourself an enjoyable reason to get up, and make the most of this time. After a few days, set the alarm 15 minutes earlier still. Repeat until you reach your target wake-up time; small steps are the way to change a habit.

WHEN TO DO IT

Do this every day for 30 days. By repeatedly finding rewards for getting up earlier, you'll be perkier during the day and naturally want to sleep earlier at night. Make sure you stick to the same bedtime too.

10 CALMING COLOR

If you find it hard to wind down in the evening, don't just switch on the television. Instead, try a mindful activity such as coloring. Because you have to pay attention to what you are doing, coloring has a naturally relaxing effect on you. It is a kind of focused meditation on the page.

WHEN TO DO IT

Make coloring part of your evening routine. Half an hour of coloring can be an effective way to soothe the mind before bedtime. You can do it at any time of day as a stress reliever.

1 Find somewhere comfortable to sit—at a table is best, but you can color on the sofa if you have a clipboard or large book that you can lean on. You can color directly into this book or, if you prefer to keep the book pristine, you can photocopy the designs.

2 Choose your coloring tools—felt pens, gel pens, color pencils. If you are coloring directly into this book, place a piece of paper behind the design before you start so the colors don't bleed through.

3 Take it slowly. The aim is to enjoy the process, rather than rushing to finish the job. Choose beautiful colors that please you—be inspired by this bright field of sunflowers under a rainbow.

Turn the page: try the coloring exercise overleaf

GETTING
TO SLEEP

The evening is your gateway to sleep—and if you have a manic evening then your rest will be disrupted. Being tired and being ready for sleep aren't the same thing; you can be both tired and wired at the same time, a bad combination. That's why an important part of good sleep hygiene is to have a bedtime routine. By going through the same steps each night, as if you were performing a ritual, you will train your mind and body to be aligned with the coming night, rather than tethered to the day that's past.

Going to bed with a calm frame of mind is the best way to help yourself drift off into restful sleep. But if you find that you still feel agitated in any way, then there are plenty of things you can do at bedtime to relax the mind. This chapter contains numerous exercises and suggestions that should help you to release the cares of the day and drift gently into sleep.

11   RING THE BELL

Alarm clocks are not just for mornings. They can also let you know when it is time to begin unwinding for the night. This mindfulness exercise uses an alarm as a reminder to bring us back into the moment and prepare for rest. It's useful for people who find it hard to stick to a regular bedtime.

1 Set an alarm clock, or program your mobile, to ring one hour before a reasonable bedtime. If using a phone, avoid the alert you use for calls or texts and choose a pleasing sound such as a meditation bell or piece of music; it's a good idea to keep this to signify "time to get ready for bed."

2 When you hear that tone, take it as a reminder to pause and notice what is going on inside yourself. Are you tired? Can you feel stress and, if so, where is it located? Is your head still full of thoughts from the day?

3 Close your eyes and breathe. Imagine the breath penetrating as far as the parts of your body that are busy or tense. Gradually your body will learn that it is now time to start wrapping up the evening.

WHEN TO DO IT

Incorporate this alarm call into your nightly ritual. The more you do it, the easier you will find it to shut out the world of work and electronic devices and start winding down. You should notice a difference in the time it takes you to get to sleep and in how you feel the next day.

12 ENCHANTED FOREST

Feelings of upset and anxiety can be an obstacle to getting to sleep. In emotional brain training, we aim to create a sense of clarity and safety in the mind. Try this visualization, which is like a scenario from a fairytale. It can help you to shift from a state of worry to a state of calm.

1 Sit in a comfortable chair and close your eyes. Imagine that it is night-time, and you are deep inside an enchanted forest. The darkness is profound, but you are not afraid. You pick a path between the trees, feeling the soft forest floor beneath your feet and breathing in the cool air.

2 Noticing that you are so very tired, you look for a place to rest but the trees are thicker here and block your path. You find yourself wishing that they would make way for you.

3 Magically the trees part to reveal a forest glade, a sanctuary for you. You lie on cushiony, springy moss and fall asleep. When you wake with the sun you are back in your own world, feeling refreshed.

WHEN TO DO IT

Do this exercise just before you go to bed to prepare your mind for rest.

HOW TO HELP

Try keeping a pad by your bedside to write down any angry, sad, or guilty feelings that are keeping you awake.

13 THE HIVE MIND

Our minds never stop, but sometimes the sheer level of brain activity can affect our well-being and our sleep too. If you find it hard to switch off, then you need to find creative ways to trick your mind into becoming calmer and quieter. Try this beautiful visualization, which uses busy bees as a symbol for the buzzing thoughts that fill a wired mind.

1 Sit down and close your eyes. Breathe deeply, and imagine that you are floating. Now imagine descending gently into a field of wild flowers. You see the bees hopping from bloom to bloom, and it occurs to you that your mind sometimes flits and dances in the same random way.

2 You are now in among the bees as they go about their work. Close up, their activity seems suddenly hectic, almost bewildering.

3 So you float away, back into the sky, leaving the swarm of bees behind you. Their buzzing grows fainter until you can no longer hear it, and within a few moments you are too distant to see them at all.

WHEN TO DO IT

Try this visualization each night before bedtime for at least 5 minutes. With practice, you'll find that you can make your mind slow down in a way that is conducive to sleep.

PRIMED FOR REST

14

It's easy to become stressed if you can't get to sleep, and such stress can in turn stop you from dropping off. This is a useful three-part technique you can use to get out of your head and back into your body. The three parts are breathing, sensing, and feeling. The exercise combines the checking-in tool of emotional brain training with mindful meditation. If you practice the technique regularly, you can learn to calm yourself to sleep.

Breathing

1 While lying down in bed, start paying attention to your breathing. Breathe as normal, but each time you exhale, try to release any troublesome thoughts and feelings you have accumulated in the course of the day. With every breath, become more keenly aware of what your body is doing.

2 As you breathe out, you may notice that you feel lighter and calmer on the inside, and that today's stressors are being gently whisked away. Other thoughts may try to grab your attention, but try not to react, just stay firmly centered on your breathing and on the growing sense of peace in your mind.

WHEN TO DO IT

Practice this exercise when you are unable to easily get back to a state of restfulness. See how it is preparing your body to reunite with sleep.

Sensing

3 Now gradually shift your attention to your body in bed. Can you sense which parts of your body are sinking more deeply into the mattress? Focus on the parts that are making the most contact with your covers and pillow. Allow your entire body to experience being immersed in comfort.

4 Slowly tune into the sensations of the air and sounds about you. Try to be still as you listen carefully to the various sounds you can hear—any creaks, the low hum of traffic noise. See how long you can let yourself focus on the noises around you without losing your concentration.

Feeling

5 End this exercise by paying attention to how your body feels right now. Is it heavier or lighter than when you began? How still is your body now? Can you feel restlessness?

6 Now try to identify the individual parts that are either relaxed or still tense. Take less than a minute to scan your body with your mind and decide whether each part is stiff or tension-free; start at the top of your head and move methodically to your toes. You might want to do this scan a few times; your mind may not be able to process everything at once.

PERSONAL AFFIRMATION

I allow my
whole body
to experience being
immersed
in comfort

15 SKY WRITING

Here is a visualization exercise that you can use to release any upsets that have occurred during the course of the day. Hearing some piece of gossip about ourselves, struggling with a difficult issue at work, or arguing with a loved one—all these things have an aftermath that can affect sleep. In cognitive behavioral therapy, we aim to identify and discard unhappy thoughts so that our minds are clear enough to be able to find sleep.

1 Close your eyes as you lie in bed. With each breath, imagine that your body is drifting upward into the night sky. Within minutes, you are among the stars.

2 You notice that you have a white pen in your hand. You start writing on the dark sky about the good and bad parts of your day. Every time you write about something bad the words tumble out of the sky like falling stars, but the good parts of your day remain in place like new constellations.

3 When at last you have no more to write, you float back down to your bed. You glance up at the starry firmament, and all the good thoughts are still there, written on the night sky.

WHEN TO DO IT

Practice this meditation daily when you go to bed. With your sky-writing pen you'll see how to develop a more neutral mind. You may also find that your dreams become more pleasurable after practicing the exercise.

TOP **FIVE** WAYS
to drop off to sleep

Focus on the sound
of your breathing

Turn off electronic devices

Write down tomorrow's to-do list
and leave it in a different room

Think of something calming:
kites flying or clouds drifting by

Don't reproach yourself for lying awake;
keep your inner voice kind

16 DOLPHIN MANTRA

A mantra is one of the tools used in mindfulness-based stress reduction. It is a word or phrase that you silently repeat to yourself, helping to anchor the mind in stillness and inducing a meditative state that promotes deep rest. The use of mantras can be effective for people who dread the hours of wakefulness or are worrying about the next day.

1 Think of a couple of words that you associate with relaxation. Some examples include peace, soothe, serenity, stillness. Or you might prefer to use something from nature: dolphin, cloud, snowflake.

2 Close your eyes and string a couple of your words together. The two-word phrase doesn't have to make sense, it should just sound appealing: serenity snowflake or dolphin peace, for example.

3 Gently repeat the phrase to yourself over and over again. Each time you say the phrase, exhale fully: this will help to embed it within your subconscious mind.

WHEN TO DO IT

Practice this meditation for 5 minutes prior to going to bed. Pairing your inner suggestive voice with words of relaxation can help you let go of any negative thoughts about sleep. You can also do this exercise at any time of day when you want to feel stillness.

17 TALK YOURSELF SLEEPY

Think of this exercise as a form of self-hypnosis in which you gently persuade your body to calm down to the point where you can sleep through the night. In cognitive behavioral therapy, we take the view that the way we talk to ourselves can make us feel better or worse. Positive self-talk has been shown to allay negative feelings and reverse their harmful impact on the psyche. Cognitive behavioral therapists have found that such self-talking can help with stress-related insomnia.

1 Find a comfortable reclining position on your back. Imagine that your body is encased in a block of ice. The cold is bitter, but your body is so tense you barely feel it. You know that relaxing will somehow generate the warmth to melt the ice all around you.

2 In a firm but gentle voice, ask your body to breathe and relax; at the same time, allow your mind to let your thoughts come and go.

3 Now ask each part of your body in turn to relax. Begin with your head: allow any tension in the brow to release and the tightness around your chin to dissipate; as that happens the ice that imprisons your body begins to thaw and loosen its grip.

4 Proceed to your shoulders, your arms and fingers, your chest—all the way down. At each stage, the ice thaws with the warmth of your relaxing body. By the time you get to your toes, your stress will have melted away.

WHEN TO DO IT

Practice this exercise for 10 minutes as you get into bed. Lying on your back helps the throat to relax and promotes deeper breathing from the diaphragm. See how your gentle voice can lull your body into a state of relaxation.

18   PLAY BACK

If we can't get the stress of the day out of our minds, our bodies won't relax enough to want to reunite with sleep. This mindfulness-based technique can help. It allows you to review the day in a methodical way, helping you to leave events and experiences in the past, and so move toward a more sleep-friendly attitude.

Remembering

1 As you lie in bed, start reviewing your day hour by hour. Your brain has logged everything that happened so try to remember each transition or interaction. Think of yourself as a movie director looking at the daily takes: you are scrolling through, looking carefully at each frame and scene. If interruptive thoughts come up, calmly redirect your attention back to the business of remembering and reviewing the events of your day.

2 When you have finished, go back to the beginning and run through your "movie" again, this time on fast forward. When you come to the end of this second viewing, just turn off the movie.

WHEN TO DO IT

This is a good exercise to try if the Primed for Rest technique on page 53 has relaxed you but hasn't quite led you into sleep. It can also be a great exercise to do when you get home from work each day.

Resting

3 Now shift your attention back to how your body feels in bed. Continue to redirect your mind back to your body whenever it wanders. Can you sense whereabouts in your body you need to wind down? Scan your body, from the top of the head to your toes, to see which parts still carry tension.

4 Then concentrate on the top of your head, and give it permission to turn off for the night and rest. Keep repeating this part of the exercise from your head to the tips of your toes.

Relieving

5 End this exercise by allowing your awareness to roam freely. Enjoy the appreciation your body feels right now. Each limb, every muscle and sinew, is grateful that you have allowed them to be relieved of night duty. With a few cleansing breaths, notice how gently each part drifts off to sleep again.

PERSONAL AFFIRMATION

I switch off and give myself permission to rest

19 CALM THE MIND

If you can't get to sleep by using one of the exercises in this chapter, then don't lie there for hours. Cognitive behavioral therapists say it is much better to get up and move into another room if you can't sleep, so that you do not start associating your bedroom with wakefulness. Try these three techniques to beckon your mind into sleep mode.

WHEN TO DO IT

Try these ideas any time you have difficulty sleeping. Make sure that you don't lie awake looking at a clock; watching the minutes tick away can make sleeplessness worse.

1 Make a list of every single thing you are worrying about, however small or large. The act of getting worries down on paper can release the mind from a cycle of negative thinking. Then go back to bed leaving the list (and your worries) behind you.

2 Read something short. A poem is ideal because there is something about the rhythm that is inherently relaxing, and because it is short you don't feel compelled to plow on if you start to feel weary.

3 Try coloring. One reason coloring is relaxing is that it requires you to do a repetitive action; it is also rewarding because you see instant progress.

Try this: use the coloring exercise opposite to help distract you

STAYING
ASLEEP

For many people with sleep problems, the trouble starts not at the start but in the middle of the night. They wake up, often without knowing why, and then cannot get back to sleep. Sometimes you can trace the reason for a disturbed night back to something you have done the night before, such as having a heavy meal; if so, you can treat this as a useful reminder of the importance of good sleep hygiene. But there are also many other reasons why you might awaken in the night, from overheating to noise to worries resurfacing.

This chapter offers self-help strategies that you can use to regain sleep. Try the different methods, or combinations of methods, to see what works for you. If all else fails, get up and go into a different room to do something calming and repetitive—this helps to stop you from associating sleeplessness with your bedroom. But above all, don't fret: sleep is by definition a letting-go, and no-one has ever successfully forced themselves to do it.

20 STAY COOL

Becoming physically overheated is a common cause of sleeplessness. There are obvious things we can do to stay comfortable on a muggy night—wear lighter pajamas, keep the window slightly open, ditch the duvet—but this simple visualization, based on the methodology of cognitive behavioral therapy, can also help by giving you an inner vision of coolness.

1 If you wake up in the night because it is too hot, imagine a field covered in a soft blanket of freshly fallen snow.

2 In your mind's eye, lay yourself down on the snowfield. It is a strangely comfortable place to be. More snow is falling in heavy, cottony flakes—and each one that falls on you draws the heat from your body.

3 You are deliciously cool and dry. The snow is falling so gently, so silently, that it cannot help but calm you. Imagine that you are falling asleep just where you are, out in the open.

WHEN TO DO IT

Do this exercise whenever feeling overheated causes you to wake up.

HOW TO HELP

Keep the curtains or blinds drawn during hot days, and open the windows in the evening to let in the cool air.

21   WAKEFUL WORRIES

Did you ever wake in a panic about some imaginary thing: you left the car lights on; you forgot to renew the home insurance; you can't remember where your passport is… Emotional brain training suggests that our mind is always trying to stir up old stressors. It will fixate on stressful thoughts until we can detach from them. But it is possible to rewire your worry circuits and reconnect with sleep—try this exercise to help.

1 If some urgent worry has woken you from sleep, just stay where you are. Make yourself comfortable in your bed.

2 Imagine that you are standing at the bottom of a waterfall. The cascading water is cold, loud, and so powerful that you can hardly keep your feet. You are about to slip and fall.

3 There is a hanging tree just within reach. You grab hold of the closest branch to steady yourself, then find that you can use it to haul yourself out from under the waterfall, onto higher ground that is warm and dry. You look down from your safe high ground and realize that you can leave your worries behind you, as you did the waterfall.

WHEN TO DO IT

Try this exercise whenever you have woken in the middle of the night. The branch represents the part of your brain that wants to draw you away from the cascade of worry, back to a place that is calm and conducive to sleep.

22   THE FLOATING BED

The average person turns or changes position more than 100 times in the course of a night's sleep. According to sleep experts, this can be a problem if you share a bed that is too small. If it is not practical for you to have a bigger bed, you can at least turn to the tools of cognitive behavioral therapy to create the illusion of space in your mind.

1 If you feel cramped in your bed, imagine that you are lying not on a mattress but on a pool float.

2 As you lie there, your pool float begins to grow. At the same time it becomes lighter. As the lounger expands beyond the bounds of your room it drifts up into the sky where it hangs like a cloud.

3 Looking down from the comfort of the vast airbed where you now lie, you can see your house and the streets where you live. But the experience is not scary or exciting; in fact, the sensation of floating is deeply relaxing, and you begin to fall asleep.

WHEN TO DO IT

Try this 5-minute exercise daily as you get into bed. Giving your mind the idea of more space will distract you from feeling cramped.

23 ACCEPT SLEEPLESSNESS

As part of the normal sleep cycle, we all wake up, partly or completely, at intervals throughout the night, but most of us don't notice these interludes, or aren't troubled by them. The problem comes when we wake up but cannot find sleep again. Worrying about wakefulness only makes it worse. It is much better to accept periods of sleeplessness in a spirit of mindfulness. This can be the first step to a better night.

1 While in bed, close your eyes and take a few mindful breaths. With every breath you take, try to make your body still, but aim not to become annoyed if it won't cooperate with you.

2 Imagine beautiful doves around your bed. They are there to remind you that you are OK being who you are right now.

3 As you continue to breathe, keep visualizing the doves. They bring love, nurturance, and acceptance to you even in your state of sleeplessness. You know if you stir, it will scare them and they will fly away. So you choose to be still, as you slowly breathe in and out and allow yourself to drift off gently.

WHEN TO DO IT

On nights when you can't get—or get back—to sleep, try doing this exercise for 10 minutes. Sometimes cultivating an attitude of self-love and self-kindness can help induce sleepiness. If not, get up and go to a different room (see page 68 for ideas on how to make yourself feel sleepy again).

PERSONAL AFFIRMATION

our thoughts
do not
control us,
they are
just
thoughts

24 PILLOW TALK

Worrying about tomorrow is a sure way to mess up your night's sleep. The labeling tool used in mindfulness can help to keep your fretting from taking charge of your sleep. The idea here is to gently name your thoughts without judging or criticizing. This exercise makes use of a cushion to help with the labeling process.

1 Sit down and rest the cushion on your lap. Bring your full attention to your breathing.

2 When you notice that you are worrying, pick up the cushion and look straight at it. Imagine that you can hear the cushion speak. In a neutral and non-critical voice it says: "You are just fretting."

3 Go back to focusing on your breathing until another worrisome thought comes up. Repeat the brief conversation with your cushion—"You are just fretting"—until you feel calm enough to go to bed for the night.

WHEN TO DO IT

Do this exercise any time you are woken up by stressful thoughts. The cushion is used as a tool to help you take note of your emotional processes, which is the first step to loosening their grip on you.

25   THE HEART THAT BURNS

Heartburn or indigestion is a common cause of sleeplessness. There are practical things you can do, such as not eating heavily before bedtime and sleeping with a higher pillow, but here is an exercise that will help soothe any anxiety you experience in tandem with the pain. It draws on the emotional brain-training tools of "cycling" through negative emotions and releasing expectations, to achieve a more positive attitude.

1 Think for a moment about a cactus. It is prickly on the outside but soft, moist, and pliable on the inside. If your body is letting your mind know that it feels prickly, your mind can be empathetic but doesn't need to feel prickly too.

2 Instead of expecting the worst, release your tension by filling in the phrase "I'm anxious that…" Examine the expectations that are fueling your anxiety; they may be based on fear rather than the reality of your experience.

3 With a relaxed mind, repeat to yourself that this condition isn't comfortable, but that the prickliness will soon pass.

WHEN TO DO IT

Practice this exercise at night whether your heartburn is present or not. Training your mind to manage pain can help you create an openness to your condition without causing more emotional distress.

TOP **FIVE** WAYS
to deal with wakefulness

Get out of bed if you can't sleep

Do something repetitive
or calming, such
as coloring or housework

Write down the thoughts
that are keeping you awake

Do some gentle yoga
or stretching

Drink a cup of herbal tea
or warm milk

26 WAVES OF SILENCE

There's no escaping noise. Even at night you can be woken by a passing car, the rain pattering on your window, or some inexplicable creaking in your home. Mindfulness can help you accept that you live in a world of sounds, 24/7, and that acceptance will make it easier for you to sleep through.

1 Start by concentrating on your breathing and all the sensations associated with it: the flow of air through your nostrils, the rise and fall of your abdomen. Gradually shift your attention to the sounds around you. What are they? A distant siren? A rattling window? The low hum of your heating?

2 Now, with each breath, imagine that you are moving away from your bedroom. Picture yourself outside listening to the ocean. Tune into the rhythm of the tide as the waves break and retreat, then advance and break again. Your breathing moves in concert with it. You exhale as the waves recede and inhale as they head back in.

3 As you come back to yourself, the hypnotic ebb and flow of the ocean stays with you. The sounds in your room are less noticeable now, and you are ready to drift back to sleep.

WHEN TO DO IT

Try this visualization for 10 minutes on the nights you are awakened by noise. It should help you to drop off again quickly. Ear plugs can also be helpful if the noise is very loud.

27 MASTER YOUR DREAMS

If bad dreams disturb your sleep, try this exercise to make them more positive. It draws on the emotional brain-training notion that creating healthier neural pathways can control our negative emotions and help us encourage more pleasure into our lives.

1 If you wake up aware of a dream that didn't end well, consider whether you can think of a happier ending? Let's say you see yourself being chased by a monster or hearing the thunder of hooves behind you as you desperately try to escape.

2 Ask your positive emotions to come up with a more satisfying ending—the creature runs away when you turn to face it, or you realize that those hooves belong to a beautiful stallion that will take you anywhere you want to go. Then lie there, breathe, and re-imagine yourself into the scenario but give it your new, happier ending.

3 Try writing down the dream with the positive ending, to help fix it in your mind. If you have a recurring dream, keep this by your bedside and read it before going to sleep.

WHEN TO DO IT

Practice this exercise whenever you wake up from a disheartening or upsetting dream or if you have a recurring nightmare. Know that you are able to step outside your dreams and be your own dream master.

28 DEEP BLUE SEA

All sleep experts agree that your bed should be a place reserved for sleep and for intimacy. If you keep waking up at night, try doing one of the exercises in this chapter to help yourself go back to sleep. If that doesn't work, get up and distract yourself from your insomnia with a restful activity such as reading, meditation, or coloring.

WHEN TO DO IT

Try coloring any time you find it difficult to sleep. If this happens frequently, seek medical advice. Wakefulness is associated with sleep apnea and other health conditions.

1 Choose a detailed design, such as the one on the following pages. The intricacy of the designs forces you to engage your mind, and so let go of other concerns.

2 It doesn't really matter what colors you choose, but it may help to color these watery scenes in shades of blue, which are known to be restful.

3 Color until you feel your eyelids starting to droop. Go back to bed, and keep the image of your coloring in mind as you drift off slowly to sleep.

Turn the page: try the coloring exercise overleaf

DEALING
WITH
DIFFICULTY

Life's upsets can have a big impact on our sleep. Most of us have at some time had the experience of lying awake in a state of emotional turmoil, knowing that we are at the mercy of our feelings. It is often said that we can't help what we feel—but that is only partly true. We can't stop our feelings, but we don't have to allow them to dominate us and do us down. Our emotions can be managed: they need not be like a tornado that comes out of nowhere and carries us off. With practice, we can make them more like a drama that we watch onstage: we see what is going on, we feel it, but we are also in some sense detached from it.

That is the subject of this chapter. The tools and the strategies described are there for you to use at night, but don't hesitate to call on them at any time of day, whenever you feel that your emotions are in danger of overwhelming you. By learning to manage your negative feelings, you are sure to sleep better in the end.

29 DIVERSION TACTIC

It is easy to believe that our thoughts are like weather patterns—that they are outside our power, and that we have to put up with them when they are bad. But you can choose whether to allow your thoughts into the foreground of your mind, or direct them to the background. This visualization gives you a way of marshaling your thoughts, just as an air traffic controller marshals the airplanes in a crowded sky.

1 With eyes closed, imagine yourself as a despatcher in air traffic control. It's a busy day, but you are highly skilled. With the radar screen in front of you, you can foresee problems on the ground and in the air.

2 You see an unscheduled airplane coming in to land on a busy runway. This is potentially disastrous—but you have matters in hand. You radio the airplane, and tell it to abandon its approach. You watch on screen as the plane does as instructed. You breathe a sigh of relief.

3 Open your eyes, and connect that situation with your life. When unpleasant thoughts pop up on your mental radar like that rogue plane, it is in your power to order them away.

WHEN TO DO IT

Practice this exercise two hours before bedtime to prevent troublesome thoughts from keeping you up at night.

I accept
what I have done and I am
moving on

30   RELEASE THE GUILT

When we start to relax, guilt about what we have or haven't done comes to the front of our minds. Sometimes guilt can act as our moral compass, and nudge us toward better habits. But all too often, when we feel guilty, we engage in self-punishing thoughts. This mindfulness exercise shows you how to work with guilt, lessening its power to disturb your equilibrium and disrupt your rest.

1 Start by paying mindful attention to your breath, then move your focus to your feeling of shame.

2 Notice where in the body it is present, its qualities, and whether it is ever-changing or static. Don't force your exploration; just observe the sensations that are there as closely as you can. Aim to embrace the feelings rather than push them away.

3 Notice any thoughts of recrimination that arise. You don't have to engage with them; just notice them and return to your exploration of the feeling.

4 Continue to breathe naturally. When we allow our feelings to be, we reduce the tension in our bodies. You may well drift off into sleep, but if you stay awake for a while, that's fine.

WHEN TO DO IT

Practice this exercise as you lie in bed or at any point during the day. When you face your failings and treat yourself with compassion rather than self-blame, you may find it easier to make amends and to learn from your mistakes.

31 WIPE IT OUT

Cognitive behavioral therapists often recommend keeping a journal. Writing your thoughts down is a good way to leave your mental slate clean in time for a good night's sleep—just as you wipe your windscreen. Try these tips to make the most of journaling.

1 Buy a special notebook for journaling. Choose one that you love, with a beautiful cover and gorgeous paper inside. Keep this book just for your own thoughts.

2 Give yourself a time limit—try setting aside 10 minutes each day to get something down on the page.

3 Don't be intimidated by the blank sheet of paper—you don't have to write much. Set yourself the task of making a statement or reflection about your day. Or something you have learned or taught someone. Or try writing down one thing for each of the five senses—something you tasted, smelled, saw, heard, touched. Once you start writing, it gets easier.

WHEN TO DO IT

Make journaling a daily habit. Treat your journal like a scrapbook, sticking in mementoes of the day as well as writing down your thoughts. Sometimes doing a simple sketch may help to get you writing.

32 THE STOPP TECHNIQUE

This exercise is a classic technique from cognitive behavioral therapy, used to help us transform negative thoughts to more rational ones. Managing our moods is important when it comes to sleep because if we are unable to shake off a bad temper, that state of mind can rob us of precious rest. And this in turn has an effect on how we feel: research shows that sleep deprivation can lower serotonin in the brain, and make us feel irritable all day. It's a vicious circle. Next time you feel annoyed, try this technique with its five simple steps. You can remember it by the acronym "STOPP."

1 **Step back** Take some time before you react. There's no need to do anything immediately.

2 **Take a breath** Breathe in and out, paying attention to how the breath feels in your body. Notice it in your chest or abdomen, or in your nostrils—whichever seems easiest for you.

3 **Observe yourself** Be aware of any thoughts that you are having without getting caught up in them. Try to label them as "thoughts" or "opinions." Are these truthful or exaggerated, factual or stories? Notice any feelings you have in your body—try to label these "sensations" or "feelings."

4 **Perceive it differently** Imagine that you are looking back on this scenario in a few weeks' time. Will it still matter to you? What would another person think about the situation? Would he or she think it was important?

5 **Proceed positively** Consider the best way of responding—what would best serve your needs and those of others?

WHEN TO DO IT

Practice this exercise at any point during the day or evening; it gives you time to calm down and approach the situation more rationally.

HOW TO HELP

Having a regular meditation practice—no matter how short—will help you to be less reactive.

33 THE KEY TO LETTING GO

Emotional pain can feel as real as physical pain, and many of our psychological wounds are rooted in difficult memories. These may not trouble us when we are awake and busy, but they can pop up at night and affect our rest. Mindfulness-based stress reduction teaches that we can let go of our past pain. Although we cannot get rid of painful memories, we can learn to accept them so they do not cloud our consciousness.

1 Take a few deep, cleansing breaths and close your eyes. Imagine that you are eagerly awaiting a package that contains the key to letting go of your past hurts.

2 The package arrives, but it is so tightly bound with ribbon that you cannot get into it. You work at the knots, but to no avail.

3 Now you find some scissors. You snip the cords, and the wrapping falls away together with the ribbon. There in your hands is the key you have been longing for.

WHEN TO DO IT

The ribbons, you'll have realized, represent the emotionally restrictive bonds that keep you from peace and sleep. Practice this visualization one hour before bedtime. Those painful memories will begin to unravel and fall away.

TOP **FIVE** WAYS
to build emotional health

Replace self-punishing thoughts
with positive self-talk

Enjoy the small pleasures of life

Begin and end each day with a blessing,
affirmation, or thankful thought

Give yourself credit for all that
you have achieved

Ground yourself in the moment
by focusing on your breath

I am fine just as I am

34 ACCEPT YOURSELF

Feeling bad about ourselves—and expecting ourselves to be perfect—can mess with our confidence by day, and affect the quality of our sleep by night. So here is an exercise that promotes self-acceptance; it is based on an emotional brain-training concept of "reasonable expectations," and encourages us to embrace ourselves just as we are rather than comparing ourselves with some fictionalized ideal of perfection.

1 Sitting comfortably, start tuning into your breathing and let your eyes gently close. Imagine you are in front of a mirror, looking at yourself.

2 Don't criticize what you see—you are not perfect, but why should you be? Try to see yourself with reasonable expectations. What does that feel like?

3 Now say to your reflection: "I am fine just as I am." Keep repeating this phrase while visualizing yourself in the mirror. Then open your eyes and give yourself a hug.

WHEN TO DO IT

Try this exercise in the morning and then again in the evening. Over the days that come you will gradually feel a stronger connection with yourself. You can also try repeating this phrase while looking at your actual reflection, both morning and night.

35 TURN OFF THE ANGER

If you feel angry at bedtime, use techniques from cognitive behavioral therapy to deal with this disruptive emotion. Ask yourself if your feelings are in proportion to the "offense," redirect your attention toward an absorbing activity—a brisk walk or coloring—or try this anger-defusing exercise. Studies show that anger destroys restful slumber: we toss and turn, and don't get the REM sleep that we need.

WHEN TO DO IT

If you think that you are heading home to conflict, do this exercise in your car or on a park bench before you enter your house. Remember that calm evenings will mean that you enjoy your dreams.

1 Write down three things that you appreciate about the person you are angry with.

2 Think of a disagreement that you were able to defuse in the past. Commit to memory the thought that disagreements are inevitable but arguments can be resolved.

3 Think of something good that this person has done for you (or for someone else) and how it felt to receive or witness this act.

4 Envision making amends and ending the evening with soft words or a hug.

Try this: use the coloring exercise opposite to give you time to cool down

BEYOND
SLEEP
PROBLEMS

Everybody's sleep requirements are different. Some of us need to sleep longer than others. Certainly young people—children and teenagers—need more sleep than adults, who in turn need more than elderly people: it is natural to sleep less as you grow older. But if you are often awake half the night, or find yourself getting up several times each night, or are so sleep-deprived that you fall asleep during the day, then you are likely to have a sleep disorder, such as sleep apnea, or health-related sleeping problems, and should see your doctor for professional advice as well as using the exercises in this book.

Some sleep issues are rooted in external circumstances. Natural cycles such as the phase of the moon and the time of year can affect sleep, as can painful life events such as a bereavement. In this chapter you will find exercises and visualizations designed to help you sleep when you are faced with situations that might affect your rest, but which are outside your control.

36 OVER THE MOON

Throughout history, people have noted that a full moon can induce restlessness. And there is now scientific evidence for it. A study conducted at the University of Basel in Switzerland found that participants had lower levels of melatonin, the "sleep hormone," around full moons. They tended to take longer to fall asleep, and woke up earlier. Here is a mindfulness exercise that will help you counter these wakeful effects of the moon.

1 As you think about bedtime tonight, close your eyes and imagine a full moon. It is round and bright like a searchlight in the heavens.

2 Imagine that the disc of the moon is growing bigger and bigger until it covers the entire night sky, making everything as bright as the day—or even brighter.

3 Now shrink the moon back down, but don't stop when it reaches its natural size. Make the moon into a tiny speck of light, like a very distant and insignificant star. As the moon dwindles, you realize that your body feels much sleepier and your mind has calmed down as well.

WHEN TO DO IT

Try this exercise as the full moon approaches. Do it in the evening before you prepare for bed.

HOW TO HELP

Make sure your bedroom is completely dark by using black-out blinds or curtains.

37 MOVE TO THE MUSIC

If you have experienced a sensation of not being able to move in bed, you are not alone—sleep paralysis is a recognized phenomenon. It's often a sign of stress or lack of sleep. The best remedies are to get more rest and to manage any feelings of panic. This musical visualization draws on a strategy from cognitive behavioral therapy: thinking and doing something differently from the way you feel—here, imagining that you can move.

1 Just be still in bed. Try to be comfortable. Tell yourself that everything is fine.

2 Picture yourself playing your favorite tune on a piano. Don't worry if you can't play in real life: just go through the motions. It can help to imagine the music playing in the background, perhaps on an old gramophone, to make the image more vivid. Close your eyes and play the tune again, moving your fingers in time to the music in your head.

3 Open your eyes, and allow your toes to tap in time with the music. Now repeat with eyes closed: your fingers are moving and so are your toes. Remind yourself that this is something you can do if you ever fear not being able to move.

WHEN TO DO IT

Try doing this exercise regularly so that it becomes second nature to you. It is a way of reminding yourself that you can move, and need not be afraid of sleep paralysis when waking or falling asleep.

38 CHANGE THE PICTURE

Here is an exercise that can help you to switch off if you find yourself dwelling on horrifying or frightening images when you go to bed. It can also be used if you suffer from night terrors. These are most common in children, but adults experience them, too. The phenomenon is most prevalent when people are dealing with a migraine or are stressed, sleep-deprived, or feverish. Night terrors are associated with other sleep disorders including restless leg syndrome and sleep apnea.

1 Sit down, close your eyes, and imagine that you are watching television. Be aware that all the available channels represent your unconscious streams of thought.

2 Imagine that you are flipping through the channels. You notice that at this hour there are some gruesome programs that show scenes of killing, destruction, and the like. Your attention is held by one of those programs for a moment, but you remember that you have the remote control and can switch it off.

3 You change channels to a happy scene of people laughing and enjoying themselves in a beautiful garden. You notice that this induces a corresponding change in you: your body and brain are now more relaxed, and you let yourself smile with pleasure.

4 Before opening your eyes, you take a look at your imaginary remote control, and note that it will be with you whether you are asleep or awake.

WHEN TO DO IT

Practice this visualization for at least 10 minutes before bedtime. You will see how much more relaxed your mind will be when you are fast asleep. Over time, you'll notice how your night terrors will be replaced by sweet dreams.

39 EMBRACING SAD

If you notice your sleep gets worse in fall and winter, then you may have seasonal affective disorder (SAD). People with SAD have high levels of the sleep hormone melatonin. When it is dark in the morning, people affected by SAD just want to keep on sleeping—but this disrupts normal sleep patterns. This sunshine visualization is a natural way to help combat SAD.

1 As the sun goes down, sit down and close your eyes. Imagine you are outside on the longest, sunniest day of the year. There is a light breeze, but you can feel the benevolent warmth of the sun on your face, and you love it.

2 Look up at the sky. You can see the bright, hot sun shining down on you, and you feel it more intensely now. Your body seems to have been basking in the sun's heat for hours. You are all aglow with the sun, you can feel it in every part of you, and it seems to have seeped deep into you.

3 As you open your eyes you have a sense that you have been kissed by the sun. Even now, in the winter's dusk, you are flushed with sunlight.

WHEN TO DO IT

Try this exercise every day. Visualization is just one way to combat SAD. It's important to spend time outdoors to get the benefits of natural sunlight. Make a point of going for a 20-minute walk every day even (or perhaps especially) if you don't feel like it. Serious cases of SAD may need treating with light therapy and medication.

TOP **FIVE** WAYS
to improve your sleep health

Seek medical help for snoring

Have a nutritious diet and
maintain a healthy weight

Exercise regularly

See your doctor if you often
have trouble sleeping

Limit daytime naps

40 THE NIGHT OWL

Here is a visualization that can help if you feel annoyed with yourself for your insomnia or sleep problems. The key to inducing sleep naturally is not to try to cajole or criticize yourself for not sleeping—that won't work. Instead you can use the notion of acceptance, which is central to mindfulness, to open yourself to the real possibility of sleep.

1 As you think about bedtime tonight, close your eyes and imagine a night owl. It is sitting on the branch of a nearby tree, frowning at you with its huge eyes. But it is not silent. The owl is screeching and hooting so loudly that sleep is impossible, even though you are dead tired.

2 In sheer frustration, you shout at the owl to make it stop. But it keeps on screeching. Then you have a thought: the owl is just doing what owls do. It wants to screech as much as you want to sleep. And so you say, partly to yourself and partly to the owl: "OK. Here we are together. Let's just let it be."

3 You immediately grow calmer and—strangely—so does the owl. Silence eventually falls, and the owl flies away into the night.

WHEN TO DO IT

Practice this exercise before bedtime for 5 minutes, and in the night if you are wakeful. Like the night owl, see how quickly your inner "sleep critic" flies away.

41 LOVE YOUR BED

When you lose someone you love, your bed can become the place where you feel the loss most intensely. The techniques of emotional brain training can help us regroup, re-imagining the bed and the bedroom as a place of safety and sanctuary. Sleep is essential to healing, and this is one step along the way.

1 Find a comfortable place to sit. Close your eyes and imagine that you have just walked many miles. You have at last come upon a place that is quiet, lovely, warm, and soft. It could be a room, an outdoor space, a hayloft, or a beach…

2 Beautiful music is coming from somewhere nearby. This is a wonderful place to be—and it feels safe, the safest place on earth.

3 You have come so far that you decide to rest for a few moments. You lie down and stretch out. You relax, and before you know it you are sleeping.

4 While you are still enjoying this cozy, imaginary nap, bring this image of a place of safety to your actual bed tonight.

WHEN TO DO IT

Try this exercise every night for 30 days before getting ready for bed. Gradually, you will look forward to sleeping alone, and once again come to see your bed as comforting and inviting.

42 REDUCE THE VOLUME

This exercise can be helpful if you suffer from chronic pain that affects your sleep. The first port of call for managing pain is always your doctor, but mental imagery techniques are known to be helpful as they can release some of the tension and upset that make pain worse. Absorbing activities such as coloring can also be a helpful activity for people with pain, because they distract you from the distress it can cause.

WHEN TO DO IT

Do this in the night if the pain awakens you, or before you go to bed if it is stopping you from falling asleep. You may find the body scan exercise on page 148 helpful, too. Pain-control exercises can be practiced at any time of day, but you should seek medical advice for the cause and management of pain.

1 Get as comfortable as you can, then bring your attention to your breathing. It can help to say "re" as you breathe in, and "lax" as you breathe out—"re-lax."

2 When you feel ready, bring to mind an irritating noise that represents the pain that you feel—the sound of a drill or a fire engine siren. Try to hear the noise, very loud and highly unpleasant, in your ear.

3 Now imagine you can lower the volume. Imagine the noise becoming quieter and quieter in your mind, until you can barely notice it.

Try this: use the coloring exercise opposite to direct your mind away from the pain

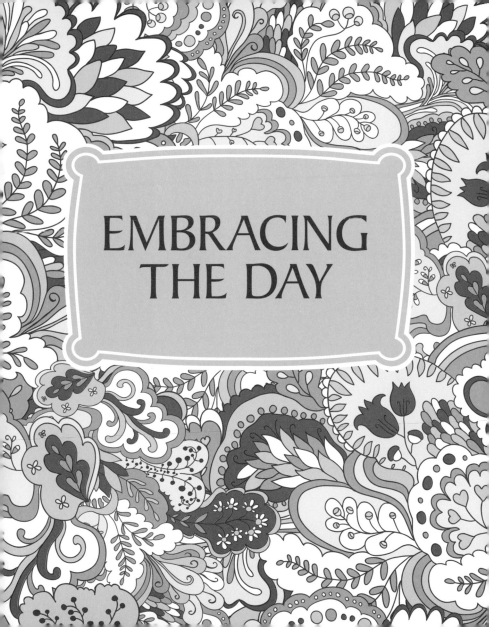

EMBRACING
THE DAY

The quality of our sleep naturally affects the kind of day we have afterward; conversely, the manner in which we spend our day has an effect on how we sleep at night. There are simple measures that we can take in the morning, and make part of our routine, to help ensure that we sleep well. We can try getting up earlier, and making sure that we stick to a regular rising time: that additional hour of wakefulness at the start of the day may be all it takes to make us tired enough to sleep come bedtime (and can be wonderfully productive).

It is well known that the first meal of the day has a knock-on effect on our eating—it is important to make it good and nutritious, to avoid the sugar rushes and caffeine highs that can disrupt our sleep hours later. And make sure that your internal body clock knows that it is daytime: spend as long as you can each day in natural light, breathing fresh air. This final chapter provides you with exercises for implementing these and other daylight strategies for sound sleep.

43   READ THE BILLBOARDS

Whether we like it or not, we sometimes have to function when we have underslept. That may be an occasional thing—if we have to work late for a few days to meet a target—or it may be that we have an unresolved sleep issue. Either way, cognitive behavioral therapy can help. One of the things we do in this form of therapy is tell ourselves in writing what we must do. It is amazing the difference that a mental list can make to our behaviors.

1 Imagine that you are happily driving along a highway. Apart from your car, the road is empty.

2 Every mile or so there is a billboard. Each billboard contains a different message in huge letters. You note them as you go past. They say: MEDITATE, then BASK IN THE SUN, then DRINK WATER, then STAY ACTIVE.

3 There is a gap of a couple of miles after the fourth billboard, then the billboards appear again in the same sequence. Within a few miles, you know them by heart: MEDITATE, BASK IN THE SUN, DRINK WATER, STAY ACTIVE.

WHEN TO DO IT

Practice this visualization when you feel too sleepy to work; make a commitment to do as the billboards say in the course of the day.

44 BREAKING THE FAST

It is often said that breakfast is the most important meal of the day—and it is true that missing breakfast is a sure way to upset your digestion and metabolism, and so make you more prone to sleep problems at the other end of the day. Here's how to change your breakfast menu so that it sets you up for an active day and a good night's sleep.

1 Go low on sugar: have granola with fresh fruit rather than a frosted cereal; plain yogurt rather than a sweetened fruit yogurt.

2 Get your caffeine fix early: if you drink coffee, have it at breakfast rather than later in the day. Caffeine can stay in your system for seven hours, so an afternoon coffee can keep you awake.

3 Eat whole-grain rather than white toast. Whole grains release their energy slowly, so you are less likely to get hungry mid-morning and grab a donut.

4 Keep it interesting: vary your breakfast. Have a poached egg some days. Or a bagel with low-fat cream cheese and zaatar (a Middle-Eastern herb mix). Eat oatmeal with fresh berries in winter.

WHEN TO DO IT

Every day! Healthy eating is an important factor in achieving restful sleep. Let breakfast set the pattern for your other meals.

45 GOOD MORNING!

If you find waking up in the morning to be an unwelcome end to the night's rest, try this simple mindfulness routine that starts the minute your toes touch the floor. It helps you to welcome the morning and add a little joy to the transition from sleep to active wakefulness.

1 Take a sip of water as soon as you wake up—keep a carafe by your bed for this purpose. Notice how the water feels in your mouth and throat.

2 Open a window to get a sense of the weather and the outside world. Take a deep breath through your nostrils: this is your first experience of the day ahead.

3 Do a few gentle stretches. Reach up for the ceiling with both arms, and bend to touch your toes—going just as far as is comfortable.

4 Focus your mind on something good about the day ahead: it is great to be alive!

WHEN TO DO IT

Incorporate this mindfulness routine into your morning. You are likely to feel happier and work better as a result. You can also use one or more of these simple acts to bring you back to the present moment at any point during the day.

46 CHECKING IN

Sleep is vital to your mental health. Yet so many people think they can do without much of it. Some believe that managing on little sleep is a sign of strength, and that tiredness is a form of weakness. If that sounds familiar, it is time to adjust your attitude. This mini quiz, drawn from cognitive behavioral therapy, can help change your mindset by reminding you of the benefits of getting enough sleep.

WHEN TO DO IT

By assessing your sleep in relation to how you feel first thing, you will gradually come to see how much good sleep matters to you.

1 When your alarm goes off and you are half awake, take a moment to check in with yourself and notice how you are feeling.

2 Run through the questions in your mind—it can be useful to keep this book near your bed to refer to.

3 Think about your answers. If any of them is a "no" then you haven't slept well enough. Promise yourself that you'll take a long look at what is stopping you from making sleep a priority. Resolve to remove those obstacles one by one.

yes no Do you feel like you slept enough last night?

yes no Did you get the kind of sleep you were hoping for?

yes no Will your night's sleep help you be on top form today?

yes no Are you able to accomplish what you planned today?

yes no Do you have the health and resilience to take on the day?

47 SCAN THE BODY

Do you wake up feeling stiff? If so, it can ruin your day, add to your frustration, and lower your productivity. Taking care of any aches and pains first thing is critical. If you wake up stiff even after sleeping in a position that supports your joints, stretching before bed, and keeping your bed warm, then try using this mindfulness breathing technique to relieve the areas that hurt most.

1 If you feel stiff in the morning, lie in your bed taking stock of where in your body you feel the worst. You might be tempted to think "everywhere," but resist that notion.

2 Instead, let your mind do a gentle body scan from head to toe of where you feel the most stiffness. If your mind wanders, keep guiding it back to your pain.

3 Now turn your attention from your pain to your breath. See the air you breathe in as healing and the air you breathe out as forgiving. As you take in healing air, hold it in for 10 seconds so it can reach one of your stiff limbs. Then slowly breathe out thoughts of forgiveness that can soothe your mind.

4 Repeat this sequence many times until your healing breath has reached all of your painful joints and you still have forgiveness on your mind.

WHEN TO DO IT

Practice this exercise for 10 minutes daily first thing in the morning and last thing at night. You can also do it at any time when you experience pain in your body and want to release the feelings of upset and tension that often accompany it.

TOP **FIVE** WAYS
to have a great morning

Get everything ready the night before

~~~~~~~~~~~~~~~~~~~~

Write a positive thought
on a sticky note, and place it
somewhere you will see it

~~~~~~~~~~~~~~~~~~~~

Get up as soon as your alarm goes off

~~~~~~~~~~~~~~~~~~~~

Be realistic about how long
it takes you to get ready,
so you are not rushing

~~~~~~~~~~~~~~~~~~~~

Stretch or exercise for a few minutes

~~~~~~~~~~~~~~~~~~~~

48 GET UP!

This emotional brain training-inspired technique demonstrates how getting up with the first alarm—as opposed to hitting the snooze button—can switch off an unhealthy impulse to return to sleep. A Swiss study suggested it is much better to wake up promptly at the end of our normal sleep cycle. Snoozing is not good-quality rest, and can add to our fatigue during the day.

1 Upon hearing your morning alarm go off for the first time, hit the snooze button as usual. But instead of going back to sleep, make a deal with the part of your brain that says it wants more sleep right now. Tell it that it can go back to sleep once you complete a couple of small tasks. Then begrudgingly swing out your legs and sit for a minute with your eyes shut, thinking about what you'll do first.

2 It doesn't matter what you choose to do, just don't sit around or go back to sleep. When your alarm now goes off for the final time, check in with yourself and notice how you are feeling. Notice that your sleepy side is now too awake to go back to bed—this will help motivate you to do the exercise again tomorrow.

WHEN TO DO IT

Every morning! Doing this exercise daily will help to reset your internal body clock and so allow you to make the most of the wakeful hours.

49 COSMIC NAPPING

Most of us think that if we nap during the day, we won't be able to sleep at night. But when NASA tested this with a group of astronauts, it found that mini naps of 20–30 minutes actually refreshed the astronauts' concentration and did not affect their sleep at night. Emotional brain training encourages us to put our health needs first. Use this napping exercise if you are tired during the day, but also want a good night's rest.

1 Close your eyes and imagine that you are weightless, like an astronaut in flight. You are not sure whether you are standing or sitting or lying down. You are just floating serenely and effortlessly inside the spacecraft.

2 Outside the craft, everything is silent as only outer space can be. Inside, where you are, there are small noises—beeps and clicks of the hi-tech equipment—but they are so familiar they do not trouble you. You float off into a refreshing sleep.

WHEN TO DO IT

This exercise can be especially useful if your sleep patterns have been disturbed by shiftwork, an early start, or jetlag after a long flight. Make sure you wake up before 3pm as late naps can make it harder to drop off at night.

50   SET UP FOR THE DAY

Mornings can be the most frenzied time of the day. Even if you are not a morning person, you can still leave the house confident, cool, and collected. Emotional brain training holds that people can rewire their emotional brains for more success and less stress by embracing the small rewards of living. Here is a list of activities that will fulfill, not just fill, you.

WHEN TO DO IT

Every day! Prepare your clothes and lunch the night before, including a water bottle and fresh fruit. This helps leave a bit of space in the morning for enjoying some simple pleasures.

1 **Get up early:** once you are out of bed, that first hour of calm and silence can be truly golden. Use the time for something quietly pleasurable: watch the sunrise, drink a cup of tea with full appreciation, or enjoy a few minutes of peaceful coloring.

2 **Resolve not to engage with the wired world:** email, social media, the news. It can all wait.

3 **Walk to work or to the station:** leave yourself plenty of time, so that you can enjoy the experience with a sense of leisure. Remind yourself along the way that there are more good things going on in your life than not.

Try this: use the coloring exercise opposite as a pleasant morning activity

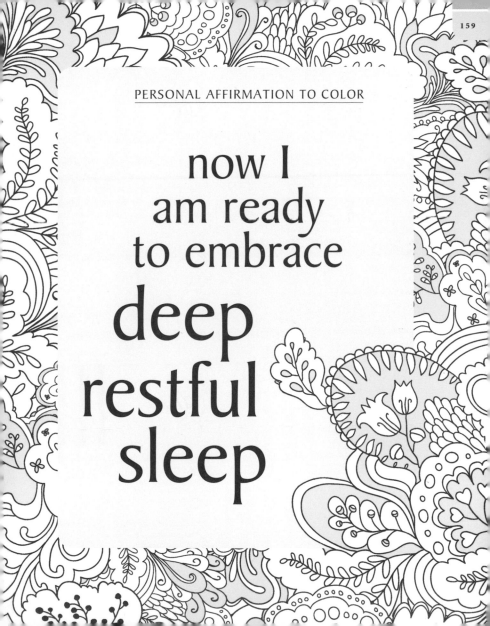

now I
am ready
to embrace
deep
restful
sleep

ACKNOWLEDGMENTS

Picture credits 2–3 (and side detail throughout book) Kryvushchenko/Shutterstock 6 MarkVanDykePhotography/Shutterstock 9 Bellephoto/Shutterstock 11 VeryOlive/Shutterstock 12–13 Robusta/Shutterstock 15 tgergo/Shutterstock 16 Igor Zh./Shutterstock 18 M. Pellinni/ Shutterstock 21 Robusta/Shutterstock 22 vitalez/Shutterstock 24 onnachai Palas/Shutterstock 26 leksandr Kutakh/Shutterstock 28 Mostovyi Sergii Igorevich/Shutterstock 30 science photo/ Shutterstock 32–33 Sergej Razvodovskij/Shutterstock 34 Arina P Habich/Shutterstock 36 bouybin/ Shutterstock 39 Triff/Shutterstock 40–41 balabolka/Shutterstock 42–43 Robusta/Shutterstock 45 LittleStocker/Shutterstock 46 Maly Designer/Shutterstock 48 Daniel Gale/Shutterstock 50 Mostovyi Sergii Igorevich/Shutterstock 52 ags1973/Shutterstock 54 nanka/Shutterstock 55 Robusta/Shutterstock 56 aopsan/Shutterstock 58–59 Wesley Cowpar/Shutterstock 60 Willyam Bradberry/Shutterstock 62 joesayhello/Shutterstock 64 RazoomGame/Shutterstock 66 spaxiax/ Shutterstock 67 Robusta/Shutterstock 69 Jane_Lane/Shutterstock 70–71 Robusta/Shutterstock 73 Iakov Filimonov/Shutterstock 74 Dudarev Mikhail/Shutterstock 76 topten22photo/Shutterstock 78 Sandor Jackal/Fotolia 80 Tischenko Irina/Shutterstock 82 Robusta/Shutterstock 84 Anibal Trejo/ Shutterstock 86–87 Subbotina Anna/Shutterstock 88 ml1413/Shutterstock 90 Makarova Viktoria/ Shutterstock 93 Triff/Shutterstock 94–95 tets/Shutterstock 96–97 Robusta/Shutterstock 99 Grisha Bruev/Shutterstock 100 belkos/Shutterstock 102 Robusta/Shutterstock 104 www.BillionPhotos.com/ Shutterstock 106 Stefano Garau/Shutterstock 108 optimarc/Shutterstock 110–111 Petr Jilek/ Shutterstock 112 Robusta/Shutterstock 115 Ira Mukti/Shutterstock 116–117 Robusta/Shutterstock 119 leungchopan/Shutterstock 120 Ricardo Reitmeyer/Shutterstock 122 BAGCI/Shutterstock 124 Petr Kopka/Shutterstock 126 Vibrant Image Studio/Shutterstock 128–129 Arjan van Duijvenboden/Shutterstock 130 duangnapa_b/Shutterstock 132 Vixit/Shutterstock 135 tets/ Shutterstock 136–137 Robusta/Shutterstock 139 AlinaMD/Shutterstock 140 hxdyl/Shutterstock 142 MaraZe/Shutterstock 144 Valeriy Lebedev/Shutterstock 147 aopsan/Shutterstock 148 bikeriderlondon/Shutterstock 150–151 Stephanie Frey/Shutterstock 152 Elina Manninen/Shutterstock 154 MarcelClemens/Shutterstock 157 liskus/Shutterstock 158–159 Robusta/Shutterstock

Cover: Kryvushchenko/Shutterstock

While every effort has been made to credit contributors, Quantum would like to apologize should there have been any omissions or errors, and would be pleased to make the appropriate corrections to future editions of the book.